This page left intentionally blank

How to Rank your Site on Google Page One and go from Wordpress Amateur to Expert, Overnight!

THE WORDPRESS CODE

NINE SURE-FIRE FACTORS FOR A SUCCESSFUL SITE ON THE FRONT PAGE OF GOOGLE

Published by Brilliant Digital Media

Melbourne Australia

Copyright 2016 All Rights Reserved

ISBN-13: 978-1536900118

CONTENTS

ABOUT THE AUTHOR

Philip Anthony has an IT career spanning over three decades of technology, having worked as Mainframe Programmer, Network Engineer, Security Forensics Analyst, Corporate Internet Manager, Web Designer, PHP coder, SQL programmer and more.

He has also experienced more than a decade of building Wordpress Sites and has an original, multifaceted approach in Site Building which consistently delivers sites with high rankings & visibility in Google.

Introduction

In the last twelve years, use of Wordpress has exploded and is now approaching around 80 million sites worldwide. In this time we've seen WP grow from being used primarily for simple blogs, to state of the art multi-sites with thousands of pages of content. And these days where the list of big corporations using WP is just awesome.

The information available about Wordpress has grown too. There's now so much to know about Wordpress and how to build a successful, massive site, that it can be really hard to decide where to start to optimise your site & be seen in Google Search.

In the coming pages we will take a look through the most critical factors you need to consider in designing & building a site to rate on the front page of Google, to attract large amounts of traffic with high search visibility, customers & revenue.

In the course of this guide, you will discover how to get your Website ranked in Google Search & seen in Google. We will show you how to develop & improve your Website, creating a structure to showcase your complete business story, covering all online content, social media and more.

We will start by constructing a simple plan for creating & optimizing your future website to generate Leads, Traffic and Conversions. This is the very first step in optimising any site & improving website performance.

The plan covers these eight primary areas, all necessary to optimise performance & ensure front page listing success:

- Create plan to get seen by Google
- Hosting & CDN
- Themes(s) selection
- Plugins, SEO & Cache
- Site Framework & Design
- Site Content
- Google Webmaster Tools, Index & Sitemap
- Social Media & Youtube
- Search & Google RankBrain

Chapter 2
Hosting & CDN

In case you haven't heard, your site must be fast! In 2016, the average viewer standard expectation is that your Site must now load in three seconds, or less. Any more than that, & your prospective viewers will be bouncing off & Googling elsewhere.

Your Wordpress site is built around a simple to use, but incredibly powerful CMS (content management system), which uses a combination of complex protocols (http, SQL, HTML, PHP, Ajax, Bootstrap, often wrapped in a CDN, or Content Delivery Network, to mention a few) in assembling what Viewers see.

In creating & delivering the site, Wordpress also uses dynamically created pages which of necessity will always be slower to load than static rendered (eg: html) equivalent pages. More about how to get around this later in the Caching section.

Given the importance of site speed which Google now places more than almost any other factor, your choice of hosting will contribute to how well your site rates, with the ability to impact your position in Google Search & therefore sales of whatever product or message you are selling.

The Hosts mentioned below all support the CDN (content delivery network) we recommend you use, at least to start with. CDN's basically function as a mirror your site and help insure constant delivery of the site content. They are now essential both to protect your hosting from the contstant flood of automated "Bot" traffic, and to ensure hisg speed delivery.

Check out the high quality, excellent product provided FREE by Cloudflare, sign up here on their awesome Free Plan:

https://cloudflare.com

Hosting Providers:

For your choice in Hosting providers, bigger is usually not better, it's preferable to go with a midsize supplier such as:

Hawkhost.com
Bluehost.com

Siteground.com

These are just some of the more useful and Wordpress friendly hosts out there, much more so than the really big ones (GoDaddy etc) who can be bureaucratic & will often make you jump through hoops every time something is needed. At the other end of the scale, avoid the really small hosts who will often want to charge for something as relatively easy & simple to install as an SQL database.

The best plan is to always ask before you commit, eg: select a few with the plans /prices you are happy with, then contact their "live" support &confirm how live they really are, including their attitude to WP sites, & how flexible they are in relation to things like site resource usage.
Checklist:

1..Check host is WP friendly, ask questions.
2 Enable HTTPS (free in plan)
3 Enable Railgun (if included in plan)
Don't worry about indexing your site with Google yet at this point, just get familiar with your new hosting environment & start installing Wordpress (through your Hosting Cpanel installer platform such as Softaculous or other tool) on your domain.

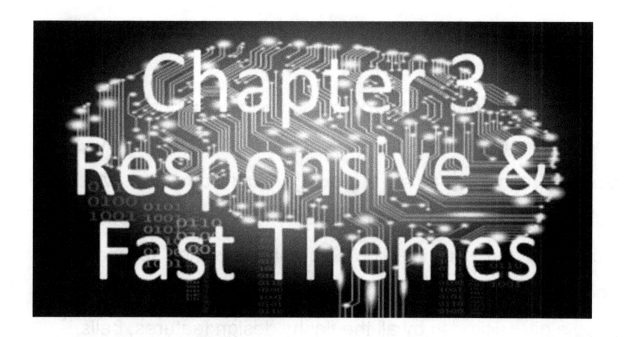

Chapter 3 Responsive & Fast Themes

Save yourself time & money by using a Theme with optimised & responsive code, which can be updated & easily managed. There are many excellent free themes available with an extraordinary range of features from within the wordpress online theme repository, or just google these to start with:

Builder Society theme ("buso lightning") Free theme
Braxton Free theme
GeneratePress Free theme

The following excellent, top quality Paid theme vendors are also recommended:

Thrive Themes: great quality, fast & responsive.
MyTheme Shop (Socially Viral Pro, Schema are all fast & responsive)

Genesis by StudioPress Themes

Not Recommended: All Wordpress theme products by Themeforest, with specific reference to any themes that use the bloated (read "slow as a wet week") Visual Composer, which will slow your site to a crawl. In fact you are best advised to stay away from sites like Themeforest.net as they sell many poor quality themes that only sell in the first place because people get sucked in by all the flashy design features, bells, whistles, shortcodes, etc,

Chapter 4
Plugins, SEO
& Cache

As general rule, use the absolute minimum Plugins only, anything else will slow your site down. Having said that, there are some excellent ones listed per below, these represent a good starting point & will enhance site performance, not detract from it like many in the market.

The following WP plugins are recommended & are available free from the wordpress repository at http://wordpress.org or from within your wordpress dashboard:

Wordfence (with cache disabled, the absolute top Security tool, essential)
Cloudflare (1) in conjunction with Cloudflare (2) Flexible SSL
Gives you Free SSL, no need to pay for it.
WP Cache Enabler   (renders pages in html, faster)
Askimet.

TinyMCE Editor

WP Duplicator (for backups)

All In One SEO, plus the AIO Extender

Any good Contact form plugin

That's it, apart from anything you want for extra functionality, like Social Buttons mentioned later, which if you have to have it just as a precaution run the new plugin against the "P3 Plugin" analysis tool available from the repository to check if it causes any major issues.

Just remember to keep the overall plugin counts as low as possible, 10 is good, twenty is way too many.

Chapter 5
Site Design for
Pro Appearance

Your site should have a professional, glossy appearance. Starting from the time when your site is first viewed, you have only a very short period of the viewers attention span to gain and hold their attention.

Commencing with your site design, the site appearance, visibility & attention "hooks" items fall into two sections:

1..Above the fold: It's valuable real estate, use it wisely. This is everything you see on screen when you first get to a site, without scrolling, is known as "above the fold".
This is the critical area which usually determines how long a viewer will stay on the site, user engagement, & if they will explore other areas & pages of the site before leaving.
Clever marketers often create a "CTA box" (call to action) above the fold to get their message right where it counts

2..Below the fold content is everything else that you view when you get to a site and commence scrolling. This is where to place the bulk of text content, any advertisements and other Info like address & links.

Chapter 6
Site Content
Main Pages

Your site must be compliant with Google current policies, including the guidelines published below:

https://support.google.com/webmasters/answer/35769

While it's obviously impossible to satisfy the big G on every point, it means at a minimum (and to keep Google's algorithms satisfied as to your site validity) you will need eight pages & preferably more:

Home page

Product /Offer page

About Us page

Privacy page

Terms of Use /Conditions page

Copyright page

Contact page

Sitemap page

Chapter 7 Analytics, Index, Webmaster Tools

One of the final steps in readying your new site for the world is ensuring the site is searchable in Google. This is achieved by the first of two step process of registering the site at Google webmaster tools: https://www.google.com/webmasters/tools

Then the next step is verifying it's actually your site, by downloading a small file, installing it on the root /main folder of your site & clicking confirm. The process is explained simply & well on the site above. While you're there in Webmaster tools, you can also submit your sitemap (generated by the AIO SEO plugin) and within a few days you can start watching the search traffic hitting your site, accelerated by the process in Chapter 8

The final step is to install the Google Analytics script which delivers awesome statistics of all your site traffic. Obtain it here: https://analytics.google.com/

An important part of your Google Page 1 strategy will be to include at least the three top channels (Facebook, Twitter & Youtube) in your marketing mix. Developing these will take more time than a matter of money, but it is important to get the channels created & started asap, thereby attracting followers, interest & visitors.

The best available tool to integrate Facebook & Twitter on your site for this task is right here:

https://wordpress.org/plugins/wpupper-share-buttons/

(based on the fact it has no additional load time for your site, & awesome reviews).

Youtube is an entirely different matter, being 100% owned by Google, & can have massive benefits for your site when used correctly. The best guide I've ever seen on the subject of creating & ranking YT videos is this:

http://webris.org/how-to-rank-youtube-videos-in-google

Chapter 9
Search & Google RankBrain

Here's where all the work you've done in the preceding chapters comes together.

In a small public announcement, on March 23 2016 Google confirmed the existence of three new Primary Search Rating factors now comprising the new RankBrain System, Google's name for a highly developed machine-learning artificial intelligence system which delivers Search Results based on "Things, not Strings" as in all previous search algorithms. This system is now used to help process & deliver all search results. Both queries and content are evaluated for intent and context. Content & Link-Building complete the other two contributing factors.

http://searchengineland.com/now-know-googles-top-three-search-ranking-factors-245882

Understanding RankBrain & Using RankBrain for Front Page Visibility, Google Places Listing with 10+ Images

Interestingly, the Google Adwords Ranking system for some time has been the forerunner of the RankBrain ranking sytem. You may have noticed Adwords Ads have been upgraded or downgraded, or simply not shown, on the basis of their "Quality Score".

The same factors are also now being applied to web pages. Google RankBrain basically gives high ranking (#3 of top 3) to contextual, quality content, along with Domain Level & Page Level Link metrics. *There is an exception in the case of Google Places listings (which now delivers Google Places Listings for Business, where PPC ads used to be) where your site can be at the head of the queue for Search.*

In fact, using Google Places, your site can now quickly be on the front page of searches for any desired /relevant search term. Based on RankBrain factors, plus Geolocation & Content, your site's Google Places listing can contain a myriad of info, offers and much else of interest to your potential Customers /Audience.

The two foregoing factors together combine to form a clear path to the creation of highly visible offers online. Simply ensure the Google Places Listing for each offer you have is optimized, with images showing the relevant current offer.

As mentioned when you commenced, you now have your Google Page One Listing!

We've now got your offer in front of your audience -make sure you sell them lots of stuff.

Thanks for buying this book & please join our Private No Spam Mailing List for FREE UPDATES & Offers.